PRAISE FOR HARVEY'S
7 *NEW YORK TIMES*
BESTSELLING BOOKS

"Harvey Mackay may be the most talented man I have met."

— **Lou Holtz**

"If anyone can 'write the book' on sales success, it's Harvey Mackay. He is a proven leader in sales. My advice: Follow the leader to a stellar sales career!"

— **John C. Maxwell**

"Harvey Mackay is a champ at sales—and he docsn't pull any punches with his heavyweight advice."

— **Muhammad Ali**

"In today's world the only thing that you have going for you is YOU. But are you the best YOU, you can be? Now a book that can guide you to be more and have more."

— **Suze Orman**

"Don't share this book with your competition; share it with your people. I'm going to do just that. Will it make a difference? Your competitors won't like the answer."

— **Ken Blanchard**

"There are three kinds of business experts. There's an expert, there's a world-class expert, and there's Harvey Mackay—THE world-class expert."

— **Jeffrey Gitomer**

"A mother lode of timely, hard-earned, bite-size, street-smart golden nuggets ... invaluable for job seekers, employed or unemployed."

— **Stephen Covey**

"He is fast, smart, funny ... and frighteningly right."

— **Gloria Steinem**

"Enjoy Harvey's cookbook for success ... It gives the reader the best of his wisdom ... truly the best kind of chicken soup for anyone and everyone in business and in life."

— **Mark Victor Hansen and Jack Canfield**

"Harvey's business acumen shows through on every page ... There's so much warmth, wisdom, and wittiness in this book that it would be well for everyone to read every page."

— **Billy Graham**

"Harvey Mackay is the only person I'll listen to while standing in shark-infested waters ... real stories from the real world with real solutions."

— **Larry King**

"Harvey Mackay is one of the greatest writers of our time."

— **Norman Vincent Peale**

GETTING A JOB IS A JOB

Nailing a Job in a
Hard-Knocks World

HARVEY MACKAY

Made for Success
PUBLISHING

Made for Success Publishing
P.O. Box 1775 Issaquah, WA 98027
www.MadeForSuccessPublishing.com

Distributed by Made for Success Publishing

First Printing
Library of Congress Cataloging-in-Publication data
Mackay, Harvey
    Getting a Job is a Job: Nailing a Job in a Hard-Knocks World
    p. cm.

LCCN: 2020947361
ISBN: 978-1-64146-575-5 (*Hardback*)
ISBN: 978-1-64146-540-3 (*Paperback*)
ISBN: 978-1-64146-564-9 (*eBook*)
ISBN: 978-1-64146-567-0 (*Audiobook*)

Printed in the United States of America

For further information contact Made for Success Publishing
+14255266480 or email service@madeforsuccess.net

TABLE OF CONTENTS

CHAPTER 3: YOUR PITCH

CHAPTER 4: THE WARM-UP

CHAPTER 5: GAME DAY

CHAPTER 6: TIPS FOR SPECIAL TEAMS

CHAPTER 7: THE TOOLKIT

ACKNOWLEDGMENTS

I couldn't have done this book without the work of a dear friend and master researcher, Ron Beyma. Ron passed away recently but has been a diamond in the rough helping me turn my writings into sparkling gems. Ron was a valued member of my editorial team due to his masterful editorial judgments, trend-spotting abilities and superior organizational skills.

My Chief of Staff Greg Bailey has been with me for more than 25 years and has made pivotal contributions to this book. Greg continues to be my right hand—and so much more—in the entire spectrum of my professional life. He has a fanatical attention to detail and an inexhaustible source of topic leads. And this is always done with effortless ease in a low-key manner.

To call Mary Anne Bailey a proofreader doesn't begin to do justice to her discerning judgment in weighing a phrase or her mastery of detail in polishing prose. She's a consummate professional with an uncanny sense of rightness in the written word.

Margie Resnick Blickman—an editor whose eye for excellence is unsurpassed—is foremost a loving older sister and friend.

Thanks to Bryan Heathman and all the people at Made for Success Publishing, as this is my first book with them.

His wife, DeeDee Heathman, helped with the cover and interior design, while keeping the project on time. Desiree Cairnuff handled the graphic design, and Katie Rios and Scott Wilson edited the book and made sure it was up-to-date. Tyler Heathman helped with publicity.

My business partner, Scott Mitchell, CEO of Mackay-Mitchell Envelope Company, has a sixth sense for modern management priorities. That includes what executives look for when hiring others.

Neil Naftalin is the gold standard of judgment and a trusted friend for more than 60 years. I live by the adage, "Run it by Neil."

Jan Beyma is both a resourceful researcher who knows the ways of the Web and a dedicated document manager who understands how to present text and track changes.

I thank Sam Richter, the guru of searching the "invisible web," for sharing his ingenious ways of opening doors to tightly shut employment offices.

My cover photographer, Stephanie Rau, brought the best out of me and managed to find my "good side."

Karen Thompson, my executive assistant, is the unrivaled utility player on our team. She effortlessly shifts her skills and attention to the varied needs of an often hectic office.

I want to extend appreciation to everyone at Mackay-Mitchell Envelope Company. Our employees have taught me a lot about people priorities in business, and you have my respect and admiration every day.

And to my wife of 60-plus years, Carol Ann, and our three marvelous children: David, Mimi, and Jojo, and their great families. They pushed me over the cliff to write this book.

FOREWORD

When Harvey invited me to write the foreword for this book, I started thinking about the different times in my career that I've changed jobs. I've made nine different career transitions, each one centered around the same idea: *growth*. Every time I changed jobs, it was because I had an opportunity to move toward something new; something bigger; something that would stretch me and make me a better person and leader. While each transition brought with it various challenges, I was able to handle each in stride because I was the one choosing to change employment.

Not everyone can say that.

For many people, a change in employment comes around because of a decision *someone else* made. If you've ever experienced being let go or downsized or furloughed or laid off—pick your corporate jargon—then you know that I'm talking about. One day, you're working, the next day, you're not. Being thrust into the job market against your will is even more challenging because you aren't in control; you're at the mercy of the market, all while needing to find solid footing.

As this book goes to print, in the height of the 2020 coronavirus pandemic, approximately 40 percent of workers in America have switched to a work-from-home routine, and another 33 percent have been furloughed. The remaining quarter of the workforce is reporting for duty at their normal workplace. In short, a lot of people are facing an uncertain job market made even more challenging by the uncertainty surrounding the virus. There are millions of people who are looking for help while desperately looking for their next paycheck.

The good news is there is help. And it starts with this book.

Over the course of my career, I've been on both sides of the job market. I've been the one looking for work *and* the one looking for workers. As a leader, I've experienced both sides of the career change process: releasing employees who no longer fit our culture and discovering team members who made us better than I could've ever dreamed. My organizations have moved people on during good times and bad, and it's always tough. But as Harvey tells me, "Tough times don't last; tough people do."

This book is for anyone struggling with the job market. It's for owners caught in the throes of wondering whether their businesses will ever reopen, or how different things will look when they do. It's for individuals who find themselves charting unfamiliar territory as their industries or workplaces have suddenly become unrecognizable. It's for new graduates who are desperately trying to get their foot in the door—any door—so they can launch the careers they've prepared for and dreamed about. No matter where you find yourself on this continuum, Harvey has wisdom to help you navigate your course successfully.

He's also offering wisdom for those who have been considering their options.

If you're thinking a change might be in order, Harvey has some questions for you to stop and think through. Are you capable of growth in your current situation, or do you need the stretching of other opportunities? Are your skills and talents up-to-date, or do they need to be sharpened? Is your industry likely to recover, or will it continue towards obsolescence?

Throughout your job hunt, Harvey wants you to remember one critical fact: no matter where you go to work, you are not an employee—you are a business with one employee: *you.*

Nobody owes you a career; a career is something you create, not something someone hands you. You own it, as a sole proprietor, and you must compete with millions of individuals seeking the same thing—success. You must make yourself more valuable every day, hone your competitive advantage, learn, adapt, be willing to change jobs and industries or retrench so you can advance and learn new skills.

Harvey understands the challenges of job-hunting, and his straightforward advice is the right prescription for anyone who is ready, willing and able to put in the hard work of finding the right job.

If that's you, you need only turn the page and get started!

I wish you nothing but the best.

Dr. John C. Maxwell

CHAPTER 1:

THE CONTEXT

IT'S A JUNGLE OUT THERE

I t's time to get in touch with the new realities of employment. In June 2020, the Bureau of Labor Statistics (BLS) pegged U.S. unemployment at 11.1%. *What an unconscionable distortion of the facts!*

- Per CNBC in June 2020, real U.S. unemployment exceeds 16%, according to BLS.
- Declines in the unemployment rate don't equate to gains in employment. More than 19.6 million workers have dropped out of the labor force since February 2020.
- When the worldwide pandemic began, unemployment for those over 55 was one of the most severe consequences.
- Many baby boomers have decided to delay retirement because they're living longer and can't pay their bills.
- After record-low unemployment for African Americans in February 2020, African American unemployment rose to 15.4%, nearly half again as high as the general population. Teen unemployment stood at a staggering 23.2% in June 2020.
- Employment prospects for new college graduates are almost nonexistent. Unemployment benefits

don't apply to those who haven't worked, so they are feeling the effects especially hard.

THE KIND OF SYNERGY THAT CAN HAPPEN ONLY AT THE OFFICE

In our shark-eat-shark world, desirable jobs have become scarce, precious and contested assets. Welcome to the Mackay Situation Room for my personal briefing on how to storm the quality job market.

***

Mackay's Moral: *When you're in the jungle, it pays to learn its laws.*

DESPITE GLOOMY PICTURE, JOB SEEKERS WILL SURVIVE

D espite all the current doom and gloom, the most important thing to remember is that you will survive. There used to be a little piece of folk wisdom: "The good people are all working." It's not true anymore. There's no longer any stigma attached to being laid off. It's a fact of today's business world.

In economically quiet times, stability and predictability are more highly valued than they are in periods of decline and unrest. During uncertain times, the ability to handle changing conditions becomes much more important. There are more challenges to the old order. Major corporations undergo seismic structural and management shifts. Creativity becomes a driving force. And ideas often take precedence over credentials.

That turbulence provides an opportunity for people who have previously been rejected or overlooked. Corporate cast-offs are joining the ranks of entrepreneurs in increasing numbers for two reasons:

1. By necessity, because the kind of corporate job they want just isn't out there.
2. Because they've had their toes stepped on too many times in the corporate dance. The potential

for true entrepreneurship is never greater than when banks are too frightened to lend the money normally needed to accommodate it.

In today's economy, titles don't carry the same weight as they once did for white-collar workers. Employees are becoming increasingly wise to the gambit of meaningless vice-presidencies in lieu of meaningful raises. Employers are tired of automatic annual wage increases for employees who perform as if their titles granted them hereditary rights. The trend is toward paying for performance skills and the achievement of measurable goals.

Today's changing values and expectations can also help ease and even erase the pain caused by working in an environment unsuitable to your personal values and morals. Who says you have to live by any values other than your own? If the personal freedom America affords has taught us anything, it's that you have only yourself to answer to for doing what you believe in and picking the life you choose. After all, what have you lost?

If it's a job, and you can't find one in your field, what about changing fields? Or moving to a more dynamic location? Sometimes these changes can seem more like upsets—demanding, frightening, time-consuming, frustrating and costly—but none are terminal. Yet some people cling to jobs they hate or stay in permanently depressed areas for fear of change.

We must also remind ourselves from time to time that America has the strongest, most dynamic economy in the world. The country's popular culture has set the standard for many foreign consumer preferences and manners of conduct. Throughout the world you'll find people who dress the way Americans dress, and behave and even think the same way Americans do because they have been flooded with images of soda pop, music, blue jeans and movies.

In these demanding times, look to the small businesses. These little gems are providing the greatest number of new jobs. Starting a small business isn't as labor- or capital-intensive as it used to be. Fax machines, computers, the internet, voicemail, printers, copiers, and all the advancements of the modern office means you can do most things you once hired an assistant to do (even make your own coffee).

Life and obligations are being extended. People are living longer. There is more to your professional life cycle: education, career, retirement, obligations to parents and kids, as well as freedom from these obligations. You have more time to prepare yourself financially and emotionally for retirement, but it also means that you have to be more careful in your planning to be sure you don't outlive your money. Just remember, as you grow older, you must stay flexible. When the old standards don't work anymore, try something new.

In this country, age is no longer the disadvantage it once was to employment. The era of the linear career—school, work, and retirement at age 65—is over. As corporations rush to shed their high-salaried employees, you're probably going to be out of work much earlier than 65. Yet, paradoxically, past 65, you're also much more likely to find work in some form for as long as you want it.

Mackay's Moral: *If you reach for the stars,*
at least you'll get off the ground.

"It's the whole kindergarten thing, Mom. I'm alone
in there, swimming with the sharks."

HEALTHIER, SMARTER ...
AND POORER

Feeling as though the meaningful, rewarding work has marched by your doorstep? In case you think you're an exception, you're not!

Current social and political events, coupled with the changing job market during the pandemic, have caused much discouragement and uncertainty.

How could this be?

Well, I have my own interpretation. Although more and more meaningful work is returning from overseas, we still face huge global competition from competent, often less-expensive talent that can be found abroad. Another truth hurts more: Many Americans aren't driven to excel in the way we once were. As digital communications and globalization change the world of work, these realities are well worth keeping in mind.

Mackay's Moral: *If you want to enjoy being all three—healthy, wise and wealthy—then you'd better feel and act hungry, too.*

BOUNCING BACK FROM
BEING FIRED

Not everybody has been fired … yet. But experts maintain that 90 percent of Americans will have been fired at least once by the age of 30. Firing is rejection. When you're fired, you're rejected big time. It's as simple as that.

Once you're rejected, you can either drift with the tide for the rest of your life or you can take steps to never let it happen again. If you want to beat rejection, remember these 13 tips:

1. **When you're rejected, don't take it personally**. Rejection doesn't say you're bad. It says somebody thinks you're not good enough.

2. **Don't waste time on bitterness.** It will hurt you more than anyone else and hold you back from moving on with your life.

3. **Accept rejection as a fact of life, especially in highly competitive endeavors.** Every year, 748 Major League Baseball pros aren't named Most Valuable Player. Thirty NHL teams didn't win the Stanley Cup last year. Last year, 32,804 candidates who applied to Princeton didn't get in, and of the 1,896 that got in, 553 never enrolled. Most went

to other schools where they thought they would get a better education. (See, it works both ways!)

4. **Don't let go of your dreams.** Better yet, discover exactly what your dreams are, how feasible they will be to realize, the most realistic path to make them happen, and the multidimensional price tag they will carry.

5. **Figure out why you were fired.** Many, or perhaps most, people who lose their job are mistaken in why they believe they were sacked. Some will say that they're failures, others that their boss had it in for them, and others yet that they were sure their career ended because of a stupid faux pas they made at the company picnic. Often, firing is a straightforward cost-cutting measure. When you're fired, it's easy to weave fantasies and imagine villains. If you are going to spend even an hour feeling miserable, make sure that you are miserable for the right reason.

6. **Don't burn bridges.** Do what you can to maintain a civil relationship with the person who fired you. That person could be an invaluable help in you getting hired for your next job.

7. **Don't wallow in failure**, even when you're clearly responsible for it. The surest way to beat a setback is to get back on your horse. As President Harry Truman put it: "As soon as I realize I've made one damned fool mistake, I rush out and make another one."

8. **Visualize acceptance.** Psychiatrist Dr. Victor Frankl was able to survive Nazi concentration camps by visualizing that he would one day give a

speech describing how he survived a Nazi concentration camp. Focus on a time when you'll be working again in a job you love and where you feel great. Trust me; you can, and will, make this come true.

9. **Focus on *doable* things.** One of the things that they teach soldiers who might become prisoners of war is to focus on small, doable things. Your helicopter may have been shot down, you have a broken arm, you're dining on caterpillars, and a bunch of thugs are regularly pounding the stuffing out of you at interrogations. So, what do you do? Focus on washing out one of your socks! That's what one survivor in an international peacekeeping venture did. The next day, it was the other sock. The third day, it was beginning to map out an escape plan. Some eighty days later, it was planning where he was going to have his welcome home party when his transport plane landed back home. And that's exactly what happened.

10. **Do some work for charity.** It's a no-brainer that charitable organizations can't demand a lot of your time when it's volunteered free of charge. What's astonishing is the number of great contacts that can be built through charitable work, and how often this network can lead to a well-paid position, as well as much-needed help for a good cause.

11. **Look for the doors opened by losing out.** Does being fired by a large corporation open the door for being your own boss? Is your company getting out of those mini-widgets because the outfit across town has become so dominant in them? Is the

way now clear to work for the boss you admired so much who bolted to another job?

12. **Seek out a winners' circle of people on the outs.** It's good to have a *positive* group of colleagues who are going through the same thing you are. But be careful. So-called self-help groups often turn out to be demoralizing self-hurt gangs. It's very easy to hang out and share suffering with people who are committed to lose. Pick people who are practical and action-oriented. Hang with folks who are actively engaged to make things happen for themselves.

13. **Find things that motivate you.** Some people feel so guilty about rejection, they deny themselves the very things that will keep them motivated. It could be buying a book or a ticket to a tennis match, and it needn't be extravagant. Working out, keeping yourself fit and healthy, participating in activities that make you feel good about yourself are sure-fire ways to fire yourself up after being fired.

Mackay's Moral: Finding a job is a matter of direction and selection, not rejection and dejection.

MISERY IS CONTAGIOUS, TOO

A wimpy guy walks into a bar and is hovering over his drink.

All of a sudden, a six-foot-six monster guy wearing boots, chains, and biker tattoos elbows him off the bar stool.

Godzilla grabs the wimp's drink, inhales it, and hollers at him, "How do you like that, sonny?"

"Hey, mister, I'm having a bad day," the wimpy guy replies. "I got up early this morning and went to work, only to find out I got downsized out of my job. I went home at noon to tell my wife the bad news, and she left me. They stole my car this afternoon. And now I come in here to commit suicide … and you drink my poison."

Mackay's Moral: *Hanging around defeatists who are down on their luck can be riskier than you ever imagined.*

ASSESSING YOUR MARKET WORTH

Know what the market says you're worth. You can't negotiate anything unless you know the market. Don't expect or bargain for outlandish wages. Know what's in line with what your industry pays people with comparable skills for performing at a similar level.

Learn what your contemporaries and your competitors are getting.

This is not about what you *think* you deserve. It's not about what you need to raise your family on ... or to help keep your grandma in assisted living.

Flirt at an unrealistic salary level? Your interviewer might flat out suggest you get it somewhere else: "Well, Waldo, I know you wouldn't have asked for what you did just now unless you'd checked around. Since we can't possibly pay it, I can only wish you well getting it from whomever. Goodness knows, we can't help you out."

Mackay's Moral: *It's not what you think you're worth, but what you can prove the market* ***thinks*** *you're worth.*

"Sorry, I'm meeting a guy, but you're not the guy."

IT'S NOT ALWAYS
ABOUT THE MONEY

People who have lost their jobs are eager to get back to work. They are motivated and educated, frustrated and aggravated. They are ready to bring their skill sets and experience to an organization and prove their worth. They just want to get back to work.

Those whose jobs are secure for the moment, but are looking to move on, have a different set of concerns. They are grateful to be employed but are ready to find new challenges or use their abilities somewhere else. They'll keep plugging away until something comes along, but they have their antennae up all the time.

But the one common theme that took me somewhat by surprise is this: It's not all about the money.

Naturally, job hunters expect to be able to pay their bills and maybe have a little left over. But this recession and accompanying ripple effect have made many re-evaluate their requirements in taking a new job, and very high on the list is job satisfaction. At a time when people can't be as picky as they might be in a better economy, doing what you love and what you are good at seems to trump a bigger paycheck.

What breeds loyalty to a company? Why do employees keep working for an organization even when there are other opportunities? Several themes emerged quickly.

Professional development. Employees who have the opportunity to learn new skills are far more likely to stick around. It's the top reason that people give for staying with an organization. And it doesn't always require that the new skills come in the form of formal education. In this climate of tight budgets, companies are offering fewer education benefits. But smart companies are promoting mentoring within their walls, pairing experience with ambition, and developing employees at all stages of their careers.

Coaching and feedback. Even top performers need to know how they are doing, what's really working and what improvements are necessary. Smart managers understand that every employee wants to feel like their contributions are being noticed. It's a mistake to assume that workers know how things are going just because managers are satisfied with results. When employees begin to wonder whether the company cares about their careers, they think about moving on. Regular reporting or feedback sessions can be brief but are critical to employee job satisfaction—even when the feedback is less than glowing.

Positive work environment. Many people spend almost as much time at work as they spend away from it, so the work environment matters. Whether it's a factory floor or a corner office, the surroundings and the co-workers influence a big chunk of job satisfaction. Managers need to keep the work flowing; a constructive approach keeps morale up. So does a little fun every now and then. Birthday celebrations and employee recognition needn't be elaborate, but a little stroke goes a long way.

Good bosses. The fact is, people don't really leave jobs, they leave bosses. A great boss provides all of the above, plus takes an appropriate interest in the employee as a person.

Consider what happens when a favorite boss leaves the company: an exodus. People who seemed to be happy with their jobs resign to follow the leader. And that's usually not about the money either, but the person in charge.

When you interview, often one of the last subjects that comes up is salary. It's possible to determine a salary range before you start the whole process, using the going rates in the industry. I always counsel job hunters not to base their decisions solely on the paycheck.

If you take a permanent job merely for the compensation, I'm willing to bet that your job satisfaction will be on the low end of the scale and your frustration will be off the charts. But if it's a job you love, and you prove your value to the company, chances are, the money will follow.

Mackay's Moral: Money talks,
but it shouldn't have the final say.

MELTING ICE CREAM: HOW THE SIDELINE CLOCK TICKS AGAINST YOU

The following list includes 20 life-defining reasons not to lose another minute by remaining unemployed.

The longer you stay unemployed:

- The harder it is to leverage your most recent career successes.
- The more you put yourself out of touch with cutting-edge technology.
- The more suspicious prospective employers will be that you are a reject.
- The harder it is to keep your positive references and backers enthusiastic and fired up about you.
- The likelier you will be to settle for sub-standard work just to stay afloat financially.
- The likelier you may be to downsize your achievements and market value to a completely different (any maybe unwise) tier of job possibilities.
- The harder it is for you to do networking favors for others because you have no official platform.

- The more difficult it will be to explain this employment gap, not just now, but down the road.
- The likelier that leaders who thought you were a bright, rising star or a rock-solid asset will reassess their thinking.
- The more vulnerable you make your longer-term career and/or personal objectives.
- The less people you mentor or motivate may regard you as a credible authority.
- The weaker your networking ties with your peers in your industry are likely to become.
- The less respect recruiters are likely to have for you and the less confidently they might consider you to be a viable candidate.
- The harder the adjustment you may impose on your family on many fronts, including lifestyle and standard of living.
- The likelier club and professional memberships will expire that may be essential to your networking presence.
- The more likely you are to dull your competitive edge and develop poor personal or professional habits.
- The likelier you are to acquire cynical and pessimistic attitudes.
- The lower the status you are likely to enjoy in the community. (You may have more time for family or for community work, which is good, but being unaffiliated with an employer for any length of time also takes the shine off your stature.)

- The harder it is explaining your unemployment on social networking sites you visit.
- The more convinced you will become that you are not in control of your own destiny.

———

Mackay's Moral: *Get off the sidelines! You will never ride the bench to glory.*

THE RIGOR OF ROUTINE: HIGH-PERFORMANCE *UNEMPLOYMENT*

One of the most painful realities since the pandemic began is the huge percentage of our young people who are out of work. Some people may contend our economy is rebounding, but not quickly enough to offset the future costs related to new government spending put in place to help the unemployed.

What young adults need to worry about is *not* how to shine on their first day on the job. *It's about learning to excel your first day in the job market!* If you're a young person entering today's job jungle, it's a little like suiting up for an episode of *Survivor* in the outer reaches of Borneo.

The job description of the successfully unemployed may be the toughest in the world: Your goal is to make your present assignment past tense *pronto!*

1. **Get a routine and stick to it.** Getting a job is not a nine-to-five job. It's a sixteen-hour-a-day proposition, from the moment you get up until the moment you go to sleep. With that kind of workload, you need a daily schedule to manage your routine and organize your time. No employer is around to police your time management, and

that means the control burden falls squarely on your own shoulders. This doesn't mean you're being sentenced to endless rounds of self-punishment and drudgery. If you're going to be at your best, you've got to have some fun, too, so make room for a little downtime.

Start the week unofficially on Sunday night. You'll want to scribble out a short list of things to get done the next week and check it against the list you had the previous week.

Set goals. To put them to work for you, they must be:

Measurable
Identifiable
Documented
Attainable
Specific

And they need to be examined regularly.

(Note the first letter of each word spells Midas, and I call this approach giving goals the Midas Touch because it turns goals into gold.)

You can start this process by asking yourself the following questions before you begin your work week:

- How many new contacts did I make last week?
- Did I stretch out geographically into new areas?
- Explore new job descriptions?
- Improve my presentation or appearance?

Grade yourself, and don't be too narrowly focused. A week without getting a job is not a week of failure. You may have accomplished other goals last week, things you've never had the time for or put in the effort to achieve in the past.

Think of what you are doing as a new do-it-yourself skill, like doing a fine piece of woodworking or raising and grooming a bonsai plant. Why? Because you are going to need to use the same job-finding skill set 12 to 15 times in your working life. You can and will become an expert at it. So efficient, in fact, that you will be able to methodically get a new job in your off hours while you actually have one during the working day.

2. **Get back in shape.** Companies have always hired according to subtle, hidden values. We like to believe that discrimination in the marketplace has been largely eliminated. Not so. Even though we have legislation that forbids hiring on the basis of race, religion, age and gender, there are still millions of Americans who have no legal protection against job discrimination. Prejudice against overweight people seems to be the only form of discrimination that hasn't been made illegal, and it's practiced with a vengeance. All things being equal, studies have shown that the overweight have a much poorer chance of getting a job than people who are not overweight.

Under any circumstances, take huge pains with your grooming, hairstyling and wardrobe. And not just at interviews, either. Looking good is the rule every time you poke your nose outside the door. If you're serious about getting a job, you're going to be visible in a number of ways where your appearance will be observed and can work for you or against you. This is yet another reason for keeping visuals of the mugging, cavorting you off social media.

We're not all perfect 10s, but there's a lot we can do to catapult ourselves up the scale. Appearance has always been 30 percent nature and 70 percent cunning artifice, so we can all be at least 7s if we try.

3. **Read.** Until newspapers and magazines go out of business or they install widespread paywalls on the internet—and that may never come to pass—your problem is not going to be a scarcity of information. Develop a high-protein media diet on the internet: *Wall Street Journal, Fortune, Financial Times, Inc., Forbes.* You can also use websites like *Bloomberg* and the *New York Times* to get a ton of business news.

It's not uncommon for an interviewer to ask the "friendly" and "casual" question: "What have you been reading lately?" Have a good answer. Current business books and e-zines, trade and technical journals in your field, thoughtful books of any kind, fiction or nonfiction all qualify, *if* you can discuss them creatively and analytically. Be able to recite your bookmarks on Google Chrome or Mozilla Firefox. By the way, I hope your search engine is at least as good as either of those.

One job seeker took his efforts so seriously that each evening he was frozen in front of his screen for hours to bone up for the next day's interviews. His little daughter couldn't understand and one day asked, "Mommy, why does Daddy stare at those dumb articles all night? I want him to teach me how to play Candy Crush."

Her mother explained to the tot, "Well, darling, you see, Daddy has so much work to do, he has to log on and finish it at home."

"Well," responded the daughter, "why don't they put him in a slower group?"

4. Practice explaining what you do in accurate, dynamic terms. Several years ago, the chief of police in a small city in Illinois applied for the chief's job in a bigger city. He was asked to fill out a questionnaire. Here's the first question, and his answer (in part), exactly as he wrote it.

> Q: Discuss your management, budgeting, and administrative experience which you believe qualified you to serve as chief of a police department of our size.
>
> A: ...*As a police manager who holds an MBA degree, I strongly believe that a progressive policy agency may also successfully use some of the corporate strategy of private business. For too long in police work, the "company" has dictated what service the citizenry will have and how they will receive it. In successful private enterprise, the customer has a large say in what and how services will be provided. This is why I read* Business Week *just as avidly as* Police Chief. *Many practices of private enterprise can be adopted by government agencies. Using corporate strategy, the police executive not only asks the community what services it wants, but also what its priorities are.*

Here's a guy who not only knows what to read, but knows how to apply what he reads creatively to make a point both about how police work should be performed and about his own obvious professionalism.

Later on in the questionnaire, they asked him what he would do to keep morale high among the troops while maintaining the appropriate level of discipline.

A: ...The policies of private sector companies articulated in the book In Search of Excellence *work splendidly in the public sector as well. I attribute much of my success in maintaining morale, while also increasing productivity, to involving all employees in policymaking and decisions.*

So, is this the kind of guy who's going to have trouble finding the job he wants? Of course not. In the traditionally unimaginative, structure, heavy-handed world of police management, he's obviously ahead of the curve.

5. **Make those contacts.** Keeping your network alive means casting a wide net. Dive into your files and give yourself a quota of, say, five contacts a day. Sort your contacts between emails and phone contacts.

I know people who send mass barrages of the same email to 20 or 30 people at once. That may make sense in a personal emergency or when you are communicating within your family or a close-knit group of friends. Others are likely to see it as an affront—that they are just one in a supporting cast of countless others.

Make your phone calls brief. More and more people don't want unexpected or extended calls unless there is a very good reason for them.

6. **Do your homework.** Stay on top of new developments in your field, and that's saying a mouthful these days. There may be an art director somewhere who doesn't use or know how to manage computer-aided design, but the market for hieroglyphics is slim! Most art directors are degreed in multimedia design or computer graphics.

Creativity is important, but so are precision and ease. Now is the time to take those courses you never had time for, anywhere and especially online, and be sure you find a way to mention how you are clicking on to new skills during your interviews.

7. **Thank you. Thank you. Thank you.** Did you have a little chat with the receptionist or with a secretary while you were waiting for one of your interviews today? Write down that name and send a thank-you note recalling the conversation. Of course, you can email your appreciation, and that counts for something. But, disregarding the fact that I hawk envelopes by trade, a handwritten note really bursts through today's electronic clutter. It'll help differentiate you from the pack when you call that firm, and it won't hurt your chances of having those calls put through, either. And, of course, the interviewer and anyone else you may have met at the company are musts on your list, as are any of the contacts you made during the day. For the past 40 years, I have strongly recommended you hand-carry your thank-you notes back to the interviewers the same day.

I can't begin to tell you how many people I have advised to use this tactic who have told me how it knocked the socks off the interviewer! It was one of the main reasons they were strongly considered for a job opening … and, in some cases, actually landed the position.

8. **Keep notes.** I harp on this point because it's so vital. You're going to want to have a record of *all* your day's meetings and calls. Why? So when you follow up later, you know what was said, what personal information might be

useful in your next conversation, and what your strategy is for your next contact. If you think I'm a nut about keeping records, let me remind you that recent generations are the first to have gotten out of that habit. Until the last twenty years, everyone wrote everything down. When Napoleon wanted to tell Josephine how much he cared, he didn't say it with flowers or send a candygram, he wrote a letter (and used an envelope).

Why is post-interview debriefing so vital? We forget fifty percent of what we hear in four hours. Entering your immediate comments in your phone, tablet or notebook is the only way to keep reliable records of the experience.

Whether it's a daily diary, an old address book, a Rolodex, or most likely a computerized contact management system, you need something to keep you organized. Start now and keep track of everyone you meet, making note of when and how you met them and what you learned about them. If you are unemployed, you'll be doing part of this from memory, putting together a log of everybody you've ever known who you think can help you. If you are employed now, you have a great opportunity to start your contact file. So, get started. And never quit.

9. **Volunteer.** Get involved in a cause that means something to you, whether it's politics, the local soup kitchen for the homeless, United Way, alumni fund drive, Save the Whales or helping disabled American veterans or Alzheimer's victims. I'm active in St. Vincent de Paul, for which I have delivered speeches to the homeless and helped their fund-raising. When you make this sort of contribution, you're keeping actively busy during an emotional downturn in your life.

10. **Get ready for tomorrow.** Clothes in shape? Appointments confirmed? Schedule set? Sign off. You've had a busy day.

Mackay's Moral: Take unemployment as seriously as you should, and you'll pray for a job so you can have a breather again!

REJECTION: BULLETPROOF YOUR PSYCHE

Quitters are never winners.

There are three things you must do to be successful:

1. Don't quit.
2. Don't quit.
3. Don't quit.

When I graduated from the University of Minnesota in 1954, I was kind of cocky and thought I knew it all. I thought I'd be able to start at the top and work my way up.

I started as an envelope salesman. My first boss threw the Yellow Pages at me, saying, "Lotsa luck, kid." I just couldn't make a sale. One day I asked an old grizzly, "Sid, how many times do you call on a prospect before you just give up?"

And he answered, "It depends on which one of us dies first." I'm constantly asked what I think is the secret of success. Well, it's a lot of things, but, as I've said, here's what is at the top of my list:

1. You need to be a hungry fighter.
2. A hungry fighter *never* quits.

I've learned over the years that success is largely hanging on after others have let go.

When you study the truly successful people, you'll see that they may have made plenty of mistakes, but when they were knocked down, they kept getting up ... and up ... and up. Like Robert Downey's *Iron Man* character Tony Stark with his power armor, they keep going ... and going ... and going.

What's most amazing? Stars who rise up from a wallop to the breadbasket don't stay slouched over. Many go on to tower over their professions:

- Michael Jordan was cut from his high school basketball team.
- Henry Ford failed and went broke five times before he finally succeeded.
- Ernest Hemingway is said to have revised *The Old Man and the Sea* manuscript 80 times before submitting it for publication.

Career success is like sales success: It's getting up more than you fall down.

Michael Jordan's heir apparent in modern basketball is LeBron James. Time and again, James has been accused of not coming through in the clutch. Time after time, as in a triumphant Game 7 of the 2013 NBA playoffs, James has proven that a combo of 100% resilience and 0% body fat really works. "You can't be afraid to fail. It's the only way you succeed," James maintains. "You're not gonna succeed all the time, and I know that."

I love the story about the high school basketball coach who was attempting to motivate his players to persevere through a difficult season. Halfway through the season, he stood before the team and said, "Did Michael Jordan ever quit?"

The team responded, "No!"

He yelled, "What about the Wright brothers? Did they ever give up?"

"No!" hollered back the team.

"Did Muhammad Ali ever quit?"

Again, the team yelled, "No!"

"Did Elmer McAllister ever quit?"

There was a long silence.

Finally, one player was bold enough to ask, "Who's Elmer McAllister? We've never heard of him."

The coach snapped back, "Of course you've never heard of him—he quit!"

Even Babe Ruth, considered by sports historians to be the greatest baseball player of all time, failed on many occasions. He struck out 1,330 times.

Or how about Brett Favre? He threw more interceptions than any NFL quarterback in history, yet he also held the record for more touchdown passes than any quarterback in NFL history until Peyton Manning came along.

———

Mackay's Moral: Big shots are only little shots who keep shooting.

CHAPTER 2:
THE DRILL

NETWORKING TO LAND WORK

Job hunting is a contact sport. Making others aware of your presence is still an effective job-hunting and job-holding tactic, and you can use it without firing a single shot. In fact, if you *don't* have a presence, that sends signals in itself, especially on the internet.

Assume that you will be Googled by any potential employer. Maybe you're not at a level where you have given a major speech or written an article for your industry or firm, but you should look for opportunities to develop your presence on the internet. Perhaps you can write something for a volunteer community organization or your church. Maybe a distinguished mentor of yours has passed away and the website dedicated to him or her asks for people who have known or been influenced by this person to send a tribute that would be posted on the website. As I indicate elsewhere, the web is not an adolescent playground—a cyber "Animal House" where you highlight goofball antics to impress your pals. It's serious business, and the sooner you treat it that way, the better it will serve your career.

More and more jobs are being filled these days by headhunters, politely known as management recruiters. It pays to make yourself known to them. Be advised that headhunters scour social media sites for blemishes as part of their due diligence before they even *think* of recommending you.

Being out of a job is probably the worst time to start building a network. That said, it's vital to start as soon as you can if you ever harbor a hope of rewarding work. If you are employed, dig your well now before you're thirsty and forge as strong a network as you possibly can. Here are some tips on how to build contacts and to make those contacts pay off:

1. **Make your annual convention or trade show appearance more than a junket.** Headhunters swarm over these like flies on a warm, melting Klondike bar. This time, when you take the trip to Las Vegas, stay out of the casinos and pay attention to the name badges so you can learn who the specialists are in your field and introduce yourself.

2. **Scope out virtual job fairs.** And don't limit your search to only one specific area. With remote working opportunities, you can work five states away from where you live, with only a virtual commute.

3. **Surf the web and use the career-change columns in your industry's trade journals.** If someone has jumped ship from one company to another in order to fill an important position, chances are a competent pro may have had a hand in the move. Take the newly placed person to lunch or arrange to toast each other on a stroll in the park. Do the "a friend of mine is considering a career change" number, and if he or she opens up, find out if there was a headhunter and who the headhunter was. Now you've got a reason to ...

4. **Congratulate headhunters on their own career advances.** Give them a call. Drop them a note. No one ever got angry at a well-earned compliment. Recruiters have egos, too. And they're likely to remember someone who took the trouble to reach out and touch them.

5. **Be visible.** Keeping a low profile is for people who don't want to advance. Start with LinkedIn. You want the world to be aware of your progress. Just completed an advanced management training course? Been promoted? Broadened your responsibility? Who's going to know if you don't tell them? When you toot your horn, don't save it for a few lines in your annual Christmas letter right after the paragraph about Johnny's two new molars. Develop your own email list. Include headhunters. Scan and send out the newspaper clipping or the news release. If there isn't one, write a short email announcing how pleased and happy you are with your new credentials. The information you send is going into files that could be as important to you as your credit report, and always makes a lot better reading.

6. **Be a resource.** Now that you've got a headhunter's name on your contact management system, make sure your name is on theirs. Make it known that you'll be happy to assist them in their searches, coming up with names of possible candidates or companies. By helping them for now, you've helped yourself for later.

7. **Never, ever treat a recruiter rudely.** Recruiters have very long memories. The recruiter you dump

on today could be the person you're calling tomorrow or next week for help in finding a job. Do you think that person will be eager to return your call after you've banged the phone down in his or her ear, or given him or her a brusque buzz off to an email inquiry? (On the other hand, be careful how you respond to a cold email inquiry from someone you've never met. Are you really sure who will be getting the message on the other end?) There's always another candidate. Burn your bridges and you're going to be looking for a life raft.

Mackay's Moral: *Your goal in the contact sport of job hunting is scoring a TD ... not getting sacked.*

LOOK BEYOND HUMAN RESOURCES TO FIND A JOB

A big stack of my mail comes from frustrated people who have tried very hard to find jobs without success. With the slow economic recovery, it's still mighty tough out there.

As I did my research for this book, I frequently heard concerns from people who were upset at human resources departments. One person said that of the more than 300 résumés he's sent out for jobs for which he was qualified, he's only heard from 17, positive or negative. He was hoping for some better feedback so he could improve his employment odds.

HR people don't deserve the bad rap. Let me shed a little light on the subject. First, you have to realize that human resources is not a profit center and because of that, they will often be short-staffed. When cuts occur, human resources is among the first to be hit.

For example, here at MackayMitchell Envelope Company, we have one HR manager to service our two plants. Our company recently received 900 applications for one position. And that was through email alone. There were hundreds of applications sent through the mail, as well.

Being an envelope guy, it pains me to say this, but my advice is to always email your résumé. It's much easier to get a response. You will seldom get a response if you mail your résumé. Don't sabotage your chances, because the amount of paperwork that is handled by human resources is astounding.

Be aware that big companies have software that scans résumés for key words, so use language that computes. Use key words in your résumé that tie in with the requirements of the position. You may need to tailor your résumé for each job. Be specific and clear about your credentials. Don't send out résumés blindly. Write to make sense to both the software and a human reader. At some point, you will need to win the hearts and minds of real human beings.

Always try to differentiate yourself. Don't be boring. Don't be predictable. Don't be just another candidate. Stand out. Be different. Use a little creativity.

Your résumé has one purpose: to win an interview. Focus on the employer's needs, not yours.

If you are fortunate enough to get a job interview, pay particular attention to how your résumé is read and physically handled by an interviewer.

- If the description of a particular phase of your career or some other section of your résumé is constantly being questioned, you almost certainly need to improve the statement. Listen carefully. It's not enough to know that something is troubling people. You need to find out *what in particular* is bothering them.

- Do readers find it hard to follow the organization of your résumé? Are they constantly jumping between pages or paragraphs when they read it?

- Do interviewers find the language hard to penetrate? In an interview, are you constantly being asked to restate what you are saying? In particular, do they take your description of a position and restate it in terminology which uses more mainstream language?
- Is the information clearly laid out and presented in an appealing and inviting way?

If you lose out in a search, find out as much as you can about the person who won the job. Perhaps HR staff or a recruiter will be willing to share the qualifications of the successful candidate.

The great dilemma is that you are unlikely to find out you have a poor résumé because, if it's bad, you won't get an interview in the first place.

In addition, in these times HR staffs are overwhelmed with requests from people who are just looking for jobs to meet unemployment requirements. HR personnel want serious candidates who meet the job criteria.

Remember, too, that HR departments have many other functions besides screening and hiring candidates. They must also focus on benefits management, staffing issues and compliance with state and federal rules, among other duties.

My #1 piece of advice is to try to find the person doing the hiring in the company and contact him or her. You will still have to eventually go through HR, but if you can get someone to shepherd your application/résumé, you have a much better chance of landing the job.

Mackay's Moral: *The purpose of your résumé is to enable you to resume work.*

Victoria Roberts

"If you want a positive outlook, you're going to have to turn your chair around, Walter."

MONETIZING FAVORS

C onversations nearly identical to the two I summarize below have happened in your community in the last six months. *I guarantee it.* And it didn't take a phone tap from the CIA to learn about them:

- "You say that our Cindy was absolutely Cracker Jack in helping your daughter Anne learn how to program basic computer code? I'm delighted! You know, Cindy graduates next year and there's one thing she wants more than any other: an internship at Bobbin & Birdwhistle. Cindy's been toying with some algorithms that might revolutionize the ad industry. Since you're part of the C-Suite team at B&B, maybe you could help Cindy inch her toe in the door."

- "Hey, Ted, your wife Margie is doing an incredible job of getting this shelter for battered women off the ground. It will take a day or two of concentrated time and expertise to organize a charter and first-class fund-raising campaign to give this cause real standing. Let me do it for you. For nothing. What might I want in return, you ask? You're a gifted HR exec, and I need serious help polishing my résumé and thinking through a job interview strategy. It's been years since I've been in the job market, but I think the time is right to do a little shopping around. I need a seasoned pro to spend maybe half a day with me to fine-tune my package. What do you think?"

Many people, and that includes me, cut these kinds of deals every day. Sometimes you have to be a little more direct than others to get the ball rolling. The effort can be more than worth the risk. Just remember a few rules:

- If the suggestion proves awkward, be prepared to back down rather than bulldoze down a dangerous path. Don't torch the contact simply for the sake of the favor.
- Do *exactly* what you say you'll do. Better yet: Cheerfully under-promise and over-deliver.
- Do your darndest to make sure the exchange of favors pays off if you or someone you love lands a job. Keep your end of the bargain.

———

Mackay's Moral: *In job hunting, barter can be the best way to bring home the bacon.*

RE-CERTIFYING YOUR CREDENTIALS

R esponding to a column of mine in the *Washington Examiner*, Alexis Chng-Castor, marketing coordinator of the HR Certification Institute, pointed out the increasing importance of certification in the human resources field. Certification is a "résumé sorter" that gives a candidate an extra edge in tough economic times. There are countless certification paths and options:

- Learn what certifications are typically required for job openings you are hoping to fill, and *why* the certification is deemed important to your job skills. (Also, learn if a certain certifying organization is preferred over others in the field.)
- Talk with people who have gone through the certifying program and exams to learn what the biggest challenges and difficulties might be.
- Be sure your present certification is not out-of-date.
- High-technology fields change rapidly. What kind of continuing certification should you be undergoing to keep your credentials current?

While great managers view people as people, emotionless companies who reengineer individuals into and out of jobs tend to view folks as products. If you want to stay on the shelf, it doesn't hurt to flash a shining seal of approval.

Mackay's Moral: *No matter how impressive they once were, obsolete credentials announce you are spoiled goods.*

MAXIMIZE YOUR
INTERNET MINUTES

⌒∽

The big trick today is not becoming computer literate. The really big trick is learning how *not* to waste time on the internet. The internet is wonderfully powerful. It is also dangerously seductive. Many websites give you the illusion that you are being productive, while you are doing nothing less than chowing down useless brain candy.

Some particulars:

- Social gaming communities like Call of Duty can be compelling and attract millions of avid fans, but do you really have the time for this sort of distraction? Nor are you likely to poker your way to your retirement. Be aware that online gambling is now estimated to be a nearly $50 billion industry. Do you really have the spare change to become one of its customers? (You know the adage: The quickest way to make a small fortune betting is to start with a large one.) Games are doubtless the worst time abusers.

- Celebrity gossip—what a trap! Why do you need the inside scoop on the comings and goings of the Royal Family or who is wearing what designer?

- Rotten Tomatoes and IMDB are great sites for anyone who likes films. Visit them and watch the movies they treat as a steady diet and I guarantee they'll never be making a biopic about your life.
- Then, of course, there's YouTube.

Do yourself a favor and tape a little warning card to the side of your laptop screen. It will remind you to ask uncomfortable questions:

- How will this website help me get a job?
- How will this piece of information make me more employable?
- What am I now learning about my profession or industry that is new and important?

Mackay's Moral: *It's not the amount of time you spend online. It's the amount of online time you spend on target.*

PLAYING
THE COMMUNITY CARD

H elping out in the community doesn't just help out other people. It's also a selfish, lower-risk way of improving you. It will strengthen your job-hunting skills. Volunteering involves marketing, selling, time management, public speaking, fundraising and creativity. What could be more essential to your needs than learning, practicing, polishing your strengths and overcoming your weaknesses? I would *never* have learned to sell if I hadn't been a volunteer trying to raise money for countless causes.

Volunteer work is the best sales training boot camp there is. It's free, and no one, that is, *no one*, wants to do it because no one wants to hear "no" 10 trillion times.

Are you uncomfortable speaking in public? Volunteering can provide you with the experience you need. Before I became involved as a volunteer in building support for a domed stadium in Minneapolis, I'd have been lucky to get asked to introduce the introducer at a PTA meeting. I ended up making close to one hundred speeches a year during the seven years we fought for that project. Now, speechmaking has become the gravity center of my professional life.

Depending on the organization and the role you take, volunteering will put you in contact with some of the most important people in your community. They'll see you do your stuff. (Do I hear you tickling the keys on your laptop already?)

Not least in importance, you'll be doing your community a service you can be proud of. And if volunteering pays off in no other way than this, it's well worth the time and effort. It's good for the soul. Potential employers know that people who do volunteer work make loyal and dedicated employees, so get that volunteer service into your résumé, and, if you can, make offhand mention of it in your interviews, but don't boast about it.

Mackay's Moral: *The greater you give, the better you get.*

PUTTING SOCIAL MEDIA
TO WORK

D o you think of yourself as a research subject? Once
you enter the job market, you become other people's
homework.

People hire people they trust and like. No matter how
objective we think we are, we are drawn to people with
shared values and interests. We are more comfortable with
people who share mutual personal and professional connections. We don't recommend or hire shadowy characters
with blotchy, checkered web profiles.

It's never been easier to nail the answer to the question
"What is this person really like?" And believe me, anyone
can and will find out. Google, LinkedIn and Facebook are
the universal first stops in web searches.

Why? Precisely because it reveals the personal side some
naïve folks think they can hide. Many people believe that
what they post on LinkedIn and Facebook is private. "Isn't
my personal information only searchable and viewable by
those who have been invited into my network?" Dream
on. And you say you've polished up your Facebook pitch?
That's less than half the story.

What's the buzz that others have to say about you?

Sam Richter, president of SBR Worldwide, bestselling author, and Hall-of-Fame speaker, regularly briefs

me on the hottest internet trends. Among your network of contacts, I strongly recommend you nurture a contact with someone who has considerable technical smarts. These are the oracles of our digital age, and they can help you stay on top of wildly gyrating new technology.

Take LinkedIn and the domain of social media as one very important segment. LinkedIn is one of the most powerful business research tools for hiring specialists, to some degree even surpassing Google in its ability to help you find information on executives and other businesspeople. LinkedIn has about 700 million acquired users, and its membership is growing every day! Understanding the power of LinkedIn is critical to your business and personal success.

LinkedIn helps you build a virtual network of business executives:

- Who know you (your first-level connections),
- Plus a network of executives who know the people who know you (your second-level connections)
- And a network of people who know the people who know the people who know you (your third-level connections).

The network multiplication can be a nonstop snowball. Once you're registered, you invite people into your network. As people accept your invitations and you accept theirs, everyone's network is shared.

Better to be on the inside of social media networks spawning information about yourself than to be the powerless pawn of information about you. And always remember when you disclose facts about yourself: It's possible for others outside your network to find your information. Do you really want prospective business partners to read about your political beliefs, learn what you had for breakfast this morning or see that July 4th party photo of you in the red bathing suit? Before you post anything on the internet, ask yourself: "How would I feel if this appeared on the front page of tomorrow's newspaper?"

Mackay's Moral: What makes the web possible is all about technology. What makes the web powerful is all about psychology.

CHAPTER 3:
YOUR PITCH

BODY OF EVIDENCE: MERCHANDISE YOUR ACHIEVEMENTS

John Chambers, the CEO of IT giant Cisco, was once interviewed by the *New York Times*. He was asked to share the questions he asked a job candidate. His most interesting one:

> "Who are the best people you recruited and developed and where are they now?"

Everyone gives lip service to people being the biggest resource in business. Who doesn't sing the praises of smart hiring and management development? Chambers is saying *prove it*. This challenge works for any level of management in any company.

Does Chambers' question apply to young people who are entering the job market? Why shouldn't it? If you ran the student newspaper or the debating society, how did you help develop the next editor or the chief debater who succeeded you?

If your next job interviewer doesn't ask you the Chambers question, and you have had stellar results in finding and growing people, make it a major selling point. And, if you don't have a meaningful answer to the question, then make your own recruitment and development skills a #1 priority when you land your next job.

The people who build companies are the people who build people.

Mackay's Moral: *Nothing boasts of your quality louder than the achievements of the people you trained.*

RÉSUMÉS THAT RESUME EMPLOYMENT

C ompanies are being hit with a barrage of résumés that makes Hurricanes Katrina and Maria feel like gentle ocean breezes.

How are they responding?

How did you think they would respond?

They're screening out the clutter and using software programs to do it. Until you jump the hurdle and prove you are a meaningful applicant, your résumé is about as unwelcome as the latest batch of pollen on a hay-fever sufferer's windowsill.

The selection programs used by companies can trim the candidate list down to any dimensions. The slice of choice: Extra Lean. The key is how do you become an "ace candidate?"

- Be specific and clear about your credentials.
- Use terminology to describe your experiences that is generally well understood and accepted within your profession.
- Don't "send out résumés blindly … [T]his 'spray and pray' technique is not an effective strategy," says CEO of career management firm Chandler Hill Partners, Sarah Hightower Hill.

- And write to "make sense to both the software and a human reader." At some point, you will need to win the hearts and minds of real human beings. If your résumé comes across as letter-perfect for a code specialist at CIA HQ, there are few jobs for which you are a perfect fit. Most of them, as you can guess, deal with machines, not people.

A smart résumé breaks the code of automated screening without breaking the backbone of real-world experience.

Monster.com is a humungous employment website with over a million job postings at any time and over 1 million résumés. They also know a thing or two about writing successful résumés.

Take a read on avoiding résumé-writing mistakes at monster.com, "The 10 Worst Résumé Mistakes to Avoid."

Peter Vogt, Monster senior contributing writer, offers some blue-chip advice, including:

- Don't be short on specifics. "Employers need to understand what you've done and accomplished." That means briefly and exactly citing details such as how many people you managed and what programs you implemented.
- Avoid the "one-size-fits-all" résumé. People apply for different kinds of jobs, and that's fine. But make sure you tailor your stance. "Employers want you to write a résumé specifically for them." An organization is out to hire someone for a particular job, not an all-purpose player.

- Don't emphasize "duties" instead of "accomplishments." What you were responsible for isn't the focus. What specifically did you *achieve*, and, if you're a manager, through whom?
- Vogt offers a powerful style pointer. Write with "action verbs." Businesses want talents who establish, de-bug, launch, pioneer … You get the idea. People who administer, coordinate or liaison can sound like a true snooze.

———

Mackay's Moral: *Résumé writing requires rock-ribbed realism. A résumé's loftiest purpose is as a meal ticket to **resume** work.*

ASSEMBLE YOUR
ELEVATOR PITCH

In my opinion, the evolution in communications is unstoppable. Serve it up short and sweet:

- The business model is overtaking the business plan.
- The elevator pitch is obsoleting the résumé.

The term "elevator pitch" describes a conversation with someone you happen to meet in an elevator and want to influence. An elevator pitch should be a short-paragraph long and cut to the heart of what you're all about—while leaving the person who hears it yearning to learn more about you.

The following is an elevator pitch for an imaginary sales rep named Sandy at a totally invented company:

> Hi, my name is Sandy Schultz, and I'm sales manager for MegaBounce CyberSprings in Cedar Rapids. We're the #1 supplier of jet propulsion additives for NASA. Our global revenues have grown 327% in five years, and I consider myself lucky to have built our sales team from the ground up. By the way, we just patented crushed chalk that simulates LeBron James' pre-game ritual but stays up in the air 15 seconds

longer. Here's my card. Call or message me anytime except next week. That's when I take my annual fitness trek from the CyberSprings base camp on the foot of Mount McKinley.

Be tough when you size up what you write:

- **Is it 100% accurate?**
- **Is it clear?**
- **Will it change behavior?**
- **Does it sizzle?**

———

Mackay's Moral: An elevator pitch may not be rocket science, but a well-worded one will send you on an express trip to the stars.

CHAPTER 4:
THE WARM-UP

SMARTPHONING: MORE THAN THE HARDWARE YOU PACK

～⌒～

It can be an iPhone or an Android ... or even Alexander Graham Bell's original gizmo (patent 174,465, issued on March 7, 1876). It doesn't matter which. If you call on it, leave a message, and somebody doesn't call back, then you're out of business or out of a job. Your phone may not be out of order, but your phone skills may be.

You generally have to give people an enticing reason to return your call. Here are eight motivators that have worked for me over the years:

1. Scour the individual's personal, academic and professional background to identify someone you might know who could have influence with your target. Have your intermediary make an advance call.

2. Find out who this individual has mentored in the past and see if you know any protégés. Call your target and ask if he or she would be willing to offer 15 minutes of career counseling because of his remarkable reputation for management wisdom.

3. Find out your target's favorite charity and pledge to contribute $100 to it if she returns your phone

call. Or learn the individual's #1 not-for-profit community organization and offer him 25 hours of pro bono work in exchange for a job interview.

4. Investigate if the person tweets or blogs and initiate some clever input on her internet presence.

5. Discover the person's foremost hobby and offer up some truly unusual information that he would otherwise not have a chance to learn.

6. Read the individual's most recently published speech or article and send a letter as to why you found the talk convincing.

7. Diagnose a new product line introduced by a competitor of the person you are trying to reach and send a brief report to your target as to why it creates an opportunity for this person.

8. Talk with your target's administrative assistant and learn about that person's hobbies or other interests in the hopes that building a sincere phone relationship with the gatekeeper will help open the gate.

———

Mackay's Moral: Many sports will keep an out-of-work person fit. Telephone tag isn't one of them.

*"Mr. Hambel isn't available—is there anyone else
who might want to avoid you?"*

ENGAGING GATEKEEPERS

Gatekeepers include chiefs of staff, executive assistants, administrative assistants and receptionists. Sometimes they're meeting directors, publishers, or even bodyguards. They are the people who control calendars, block doorways, put through calls, *don't* put through calls, and often invent plausible little deceits to keep pests out of their boss's way. Treat a gatekeeper as though he or she were a pit bull, and you could suffer a wicked bite out of your career prospects.

Gatekeepers, though usually poised under pressure, have human needs just as the rest of us do. Generally, they are the Type B enablers of Type A-driven bosses. Gatekeepers receive more than their share of annoyance from above. When you are dealing with a gatekeeper, you would do well to remember the following:

- **When you phone a gatekeeper, always ask if this is a good time to talk.** You'll find that 50 percent of the time it isn't because he or she is either waiting for the boss or a priority call to come in.
- **Avoid calling at high-demand times.** Monday mornings, for example, are generally poor windows to reach offices dedicated to high performance.

- **Listen.** A gatekeeper can be your best source of information on a manager's decision-making habits and preferences. The gatekeeper may also give you important scheduling and availability information on the manager just in passing conversation. Don't overlook it.

- **Be specific in identifying yourself and your purpose in calls and emails.** These beleaguered folks have tons of information swimming across their desks. Be precise in identifying why you are calling. If it relates to a particular document, call it up on your computer before you make the call.

- **Learn who the gatekeeper's backup is.** Generally, there is one, and this person often plays an important role in absorbing overflow work. I can't tell you how key this often-overlooked awareness is.

Mackay's Moral: Getting through the fence to the top dog is easy, if you know the gatekeeper.

REVVING UP REFERENCES

Know if you can ask prospective employers to contact your former company as a reference. Learn what you can expect the reference letter to say. For example, you *don't* want it to read: "I hope your company can do something with Jack because heaven knows we certainly couldn't!"

If former bosses plan to say unflattering things about you, sometimes you can negotiate clear compromise language in advance.

Only on rare occasions will a checkered past open doors. After serving nine years in prison, a fellow named Bruce Perlowin became national sales manager of an important company. In his résumé he cited references in magazine articles to his "formidable management skills" and "organizational genius" as a marijuana dealer and tax evader to help land the job.

Are your references what you claim they are? Are you concealing some bad ones? Recruiters check references more carefully than ever these days. The internet can expose in milliseconds what once took days of due diligence to uncover. The harder recruiters dig, the more they find. Don't fake it, whether it's school, employment or personal references. Often, when recruiters are not satisfied with the first set of references, they ask for more.

Sometimes they already know the answer and are just testing to see how hard you will try to cover something up. If there are unexplained "gaps" in your job history, you should be able to cover them with some kind of constructive effort, like school, volunteer work or individual entrepreneurship. Thankfully, parenthood is increasingly acceptable. Also, consider a seemingly unorthodox tactic: Be completely candid with the recruiter in describing the smudge in your résumé and ask for *their* help in presenting it in a favorable way.

You don't just want your references to be accurate about you. You want them to be excited about your energy and enthusiasm. It's up to you to fuel their excitement:

- When one of your references gets promoted or gives a speech, dash off a congratulatory note or a tweet.
- If you are still employed, keep them posted on your latest promotion or special assignment.
- When one of the people you developed makes a breakthrough career advance, share the good news.

Mackay's Moral: *It's in your court to reveal (and inspire) how the world refers to you.*

"I'll tell you how I got here—hours and hours of hard visualization."

BONING UP FOR JOB INTERVIEWS

C ountless job candidates come to an interview beautifully prepared to *answer* questions. The mistake they make is they're not prepared to *ask* them.

At some point in every serious professional job interview, you're going to be asked if you have any questions of your own. This is not the time to snoop into salary and benefits. Your tactics aren't to probe for information on your personal needs. This is the courtship phase. You're still a long way from any permanent relationship. You have to strike sparks, differentiate yourself, show your people skills and be perceptive.

Do you know what kinds of job interviews your interviewer really likes? Answer: when he or she gets to recommend a candidate for the job. There are many, many interviews where the interviewers don't. Successful candidates are the interviewer's handpicked selections, and interviewers root for their choices the way handicappers root for their horses.

Interviewers serve as the gatekeepers not only of the company's personnel but also of the company's values. They are there both to screen out candidates who don't fit and to be the first to tattoo "company" on the foreheads of those who do.

Give them the chance to do the fun part of their jobs—reveal the corporate soul:

1. **Ask about the company's values.** Nothing is dearer to a company than its values. If you can ask a positive question that links the company's values to its performance, you've already gone a long way toward demonstrating that you're with the program.

For example:
How do they sustain their marvelous work ethic?
How can so many of the top execs spearhead major community projects on top of their demanding workloads?
Why are they such a pillar of innovation?
What makes their customers so fiercely loyal?

And, to be credible, pose your questions with specific examples in mind.

2. **If the company is one of the industry leaders, have them tell you more.** Successful companies, just like successful people, usually do not count modesty among their greatest virtues, and they're not immune to skillful flattery. Ask the interviewer how the company got to be so good at what it does. "What does the competition see when they look at you?"

3. **If the company is in the pits, ask questions that suggest solutions.** Companies in trouble are like people in trouble: They want solutions. They're looking for role models, action plans and action

people to help transform them into winners again. They're hiring because they've got some ideas about what it will take to put them back on their feet. They need the people who can help them execute those ideas and provide some of their own. Ask, "Which companies in your industry do you feel you'd most like to resemble?" "How do you plan to achieve that?"

4. **Listen to the answers.** Don't make it appear that you're more interested in your own clever questions than you are in hearing and reacting to the responses.

5. **Be perceptive, not contentious.** Don't show off by asking for the interviewer to act as a company spokesperson and explain some embarrassing gaffe like an environmental fine. You're not there to sit in moral judgment. If the company's behavior has offended you, this probably is not the place for you to seek employment. Be an interested and respectful listener.

6. **Don't forget to read the walls and desks.** You may be talking to the consummate company person, but he or she is still a human being. Is there a three-year-old's finger painting framed and propped up on the desk, perhaps next to a team photo or a Rotarian award on the wall? You should somehow be able to relate to one of these.

Mackay's Moral: *You may not be interviewing for a sales job, but you have to be a great salesperson to sell yourself.*

"By God, you're not a man who's afraid to fail."

SIZING UP POTENTIAL EMPLOYERS

What's the #1 way to differentiate yourself during the job interview? How do you make yourself stand apart from other highly qualified candidates? Your clothes, your handshake, your aura of confidence, and your professionally formatted résumé all matter a great deal. However, nothing counts more than how well prepared you are for the substance of a job interview.

Spending a few minutes studying a firm's website is hardly enough. You have to dig deep and learn what's important to the person interviewing you. What are the company's business objectives? How is it reacting to the latest industry issues? What is its competition doing to win new business?

When I meet with a job seeker for an informational interview, I can't tell you the number of times I've had people confide in me: "I've spent the majority of my career in the same industry. How can I possibly compete in a new industry where I don't have experience?" My response? That's an excuse! Stop trying to sell your "product"—your résumé, which is nothing more than a listing of your past work history. Instead, focus on the other person and *his* or *her* goals. Your résumé should just be a guide for discussion. Use it to tell relevant stories. Remember, what the "buyer" wants is a relevant and experienced problem solver, so *learn about the other person's issues* and show how you can be the one to deliver solutions!

When doing your homework, go beyond traditional search engines into the "deep web." Visit Google News and find a news article or press release about the company or try www.YouGotBlogs.com to find recent blog posts. Are they launching a new product? Have they started a new initiative? Visit the other person's LinkedIn profile. Who do you know in common? Have you done work for similar firms?

Know the company you keep. Before you interview, check with anyone you know who knows about the company: employees, customers, bankers, vendors. But most of all, learn the art of commanding search engines! Before, you needed to chase down facts like a Sherlock Holmes gumshoe. Today, you swim in oceans of detail, and the new skill is how to prioritize what to look for and how to piece it together. Number one: You want clues to the company's reputation. Is it a leader in its industry? An also-ran? How does it compete? Does the company emphasize price? Quality? Service? Innovation?

Then personalize and relate what you learn to you as a potential contributor: Do you have any special strengths in any of these areas that you can bring to the table? If you do, don't forget to mention them during your interview.

Also consider the flip side. If the company is in the technological dark age, emphasize what you can do to help stage a cost-effective, low-pain, fast-acting renaissance. If the business is a service laggard, and you were once the assistant Czar of Service who helped redeem another company's customer relations, it may be high time to play that card.

Apply what you learn about the company's values and style to what it implies about the firm's business strategy. Be aware of the huge trend toward niche marketing. That's the concept of dividing the marketplace into even smaller segments in order to concentrate on a clearly defined target audience. Because of niche marketing, there are a lot of companies with highly idiosyncratic corporate styles. They developed as a result of their adapting to the styles of the niche markets in which they sell their products or services.

Niche-hiring has been a predictable outcome of niche marketing. You're going to find the best chance of getting a job—and of being a success—in a company where you fit in.

Checking out company culture on the internet is a piece of cake these days, though I can't resist sharing a vintage corporate culture classic. Years ago, no male employee at IBM dared to wear anything but a white shirt. One day, the boss, the legendary Thomas Watson, came to work in a blue shirt.

"What do you think?" said one of the underlings to another.

"Better not try it," said his buddy. "It could be a trick."

And that brings up yet another priceless opportunity: Background yourself on the "inside" humor of a company. If you flash a knowing anecdote at just the right moment, you may well be considered a member of the family.

Mackay's Moral: *Web search skills are the platinum card of the knowledge economy.*

PERSON-TO-PERSON: SCOPE OUT THAT BOSS-TO-BE

Interviewing generally starts with the Human Resources Department. The critical contact and hurdle, of course, remains your potential boss. What is the background of the person you're meeting with, his or her personal values, and his or her business responsibilities and goals?

The chemistry between boss and employee remains the single most important work-related factor for continuing employment. According to CompuServe—now a part of AOL—"A Gallup poll of more than 1 million employed U.S. workers concluded that the No.1 reason people quit their jobs is a bad boss or immediate supervisor. 'People leave managers, not companies ... in the end, turnover is mostly a manager issue,' Gallup wrote in its survey findings."

If you're desperate to find a job, even the grim prospect of not getting along with your prospective boss might look like a minor concern. However, take a moment to anticipate a scenario that occurs all the time. Let's say that you left your last job, or some other important job in your career, because you couldn't get along with your boss. Once this happens more than once in your career, you are liable to be labeled "high-maintenance" or pegged with a similar euphemism. Gentle translation: You need plenty of attention or reassurance. Unvarnished translation: You might be talented, but you are a royal pain in the neck to manage and have on the payroll. In a job market teeming with qualified candidates, who's going to knowingly buy into this sort of misery?

Being able to cope with and get along with bosses, even difficult ones, is a learned skill. It doesn't hurt to show you know how important a solidly grounded boss-employee relationship is to a smooth-sailing ship.

During an interview with a possible boss-to-be, you might mention that you've done a little bit of homework. Explain you wanted to learn more about your prospective manager prior to the meeting. This will usually impress the other person and it will help alleviate the fear that you're some sort of stalker. Then you can reference what you've found.

Be careful, because a search source such as Pipl (which I mentioned earlier) will find everything from a person's home address to political donations and even court records. *That said, you'll want to use discretion as to the actual topics you raise.* You'll also find websites where the person is referenced and even articles and documents where the person was quoted. Praise the other person for something he or she did that impressed you. A way to endear yourself to anyone is to compliment her on her work and the recognition she's received. Remember, the sweetest sound a person can hear is his or her own name.

Mackay's Moral: *If you find the evidence, the freshest bouquet you can deliver in the Digital Age is: "They're saying some awfully nice stuff about you on the web."*

"On the Internet, nobody knows you're a dog."

CHAPTER 5:

GAME DAY

WHY (AND WHICH)
APPEARANCES MATTER

With so many employees working from home, a "company dress code" has taken on a new meaning. Few folks are getting all decked out every day, but video conferencing requires a more professional appearance. Job hunting brings different requirements.

Before the slowdown, you could get your foot in the door of many an employment office sporting a tattered sneaker. Talent was king. Overnight, job hunting became a buyer's market and employers turned downright picky about who would be offered a coveted spot on the payroll. A crisp and businesslike appearance was back as an expectation on the part of many prospective employers.

As with everything else, research is key:

- The clothes you wear—and they don't need to be expensive—say a lot about your discipline, taste and social poise. Learn what specific dress expectations go with each company you are interviewing. There may even be differences among firms within the same industry. In Silicon Valley, for example, there can be a drastic clash between dress standards for the creatives in the design department and the salespeople in the front office.

- People notice the cases in which you carry your smartphone or your tablet computer or notebook. They are definitely aware if you insensitively don't shut off your ringtone before the interview. If your phone explodes like a jarring boombox as you leave the reception area, *that* will be noticed as well.

- Dress up your conversation as well as your appearance: Good chemistry and people skills are crucial. Have a clever story, quote or anecdote or two in mind that you can slip into the conversation. Something positive and memorable.

Mackay's Moral: *In job interviews, messy dressers usually leave a strong first impression ... and it's often the last one they get to make.*

CONDUCTING A WINNING INTERVIEW

In my lifetime, I have been fortunate to know many great athletes. When I probe them about their preparation before the Big Game, an uncanny number of them talk about visualization and rehearsal. They know just how they'll pitch, pass or slam-dunk … and just exactly how they'll have to tailor their game to triumph against that day's competitors.

How do you get to Carnegie Hall? Practice, practice, practice. How do you land a dream job? Rehearse interview questions from top to bottom.

- Always have four or five key messages on the tip of your tongue. An interviewer's questions may be at the top of his or her mind. At the top of yours should always be the impression, the energy and the commitment you want to convey.

- Never be evasive, but try to constructively bridge to an answer that is responsive to both your agenda *and* the interviewer's question.

- Don't confuse the carefully crafted words of your answer with the content behind the words. In short, don't deliver baloney. A smart interviewer will always demand meaningful and relevant responses.

- With each answer, always consider the next question that it might or does imply.
- Maintain evenhanded composure. A sudden shift of posture or glance can send a powerful signal of discomfort when a question arises. If you rehearse an interview with a friend or colleague, have your associate be especially attentive to questions of this sort.
- Distinguish between a question that is lightly exploratory and one that is seriously penetrating. When an attorney questions a witness on the stand, he or she will often use a casual question in the hopes it might unleash an avalanche of unnecessary candor. Be on your guard.
- Beware of an interviewer who lapses into indifference or seems to turn hostile. Sometimes this is a ploy aimed at testing a candidate's composure and sure-footedness. Even though an interviewer may be dedicated to finding out the last detail of your career and personal makeup, many people asking questions will feign indifference just to see how you react. Prepare yourself to perform before a "cold" audience.

Because I believe so strongly in my mantra, "Prepare to win," I've also prepared a questionnaire I call the **Mackay Sweet 16**. You'll find it in the Toolkit Section at the back of this book. Complete this form as soon as possible after your interview, while the information is still fresh in your mind. Then, use it as a reference tool as you move along toward getting the job you've always wanted. Why? It's always smart to "pack your own parachute" for the next outing.

———

Mackay's Moral: *What you gather from your first interview is invaluable for your second interview ... and second interviews land jobs.*

THE CLOSER: SECOND INTERVIEWS AND SCORING STRATEGIES

⁓

Second interviews come in all shapes and sizes, social settings included.

Far from being relaxed get-togethers, these are often critical milestones. A candidate who has passed the first hurdle is eyeballed by a trusted adviser—someone who may not even play an official role in the organization. That's why it's so important to do as much research as you can on important interviewers. Learn who they feel they need to partner-in on this hiring decision.

Generally, your warm-up for a second interview round should be even more rigorous than it was for the first series of contacts.

Carefully review your notes from the first interview round:

- What questions were you asked that were most difficult?
- Which answers did you give that sounded most contrived and inauthentic?
- What questions were you asked more than once? (That generally indicates the topic or concern is someone's hot button.)

- What further intelligence can you gather on people with whom you didn't seem to hit it off to see where you can build bridges?
- If there were questions you weren't able to answer in the first round, have you gone back and researched the answers?

Discreetly try to find out what other candidates have made the first cut and what particular advantages and strengths they may offer compared with you.

In a second interview, you really need to shine. If you are a morning or afternoon person, try to schedule the interview to mesh with your peak performance hours.

Research the company to see what is new since your first visit. Are there changes in the roster of interviewers for the second round? If so, why?

Develop a strong, clearly worded, and compact set of reasons why you want to work with this organization in this job and internalize them. Interviewers will be probing for your enthusiasm, commitment, and clear-headed reasoning.

Recall topic threads from your earlier conversation with each individual to:

1. Identify themes you can build on in the next meeting.
2. Assure people you felt your first conversation with them was memorable and engaging.

Give your terms and desired compensation and benefits further thought. Reflect as well on your career objectives and advancement expectations. It's likely someone will ask you more detailed questions about these topics.

Look at your notes from your other second-round interviews in the past with other companies. Some people clutch as the prospect of success increases. Others become euphoric and overconfident. When you *didn't* succeed in second-round interviews before, what were the reasons people gave you?

You're now at what salespeople call the closing stage. The more you can persuade the interviewers that they can be confident and at ease in picking you, the better your odds.

Mackay's Moral: The closer you get,
the harder they'll look.

"So that's our offer: blood, toil, tears, sweat, and dental."

NEGOTIATING TERMS

When you're getting a job, you're working for your-self. It's time to set higher expectations for yourself than any mean-spirited boss may have in your darkest days.

People always seem to perform better for others than they do for themselves. From time to time, you read about the psychiatrist who has helped so many of his patients rebuild their lives but whose own personal life is a wreck. How about the financial adviser who never picked a stock right for himself but managed to build a tidy pile for his clients?

Not many of us are able to do things for ourselves the same way we do them for others. That translates into whether we're better at our jobs or better at our own affairs. Even people who make their living negotiating can really mess up using their professional skills in their own per-sonal interests. Not every real estate expert who spends her career negotiating shopping center leases is an expert when it comes to negotiating her own compensation. The insurance company adjuster who knocks heads all day long negotiating settlements with personal injury lawyers still may be a patsy in settling his own salary differences with his employer.

When we accept a new job, most people have to repre-sent their interests, whether they're good at it or not. So, we might as well try to learn how to be good at it. Whether or not you've ever negotiated anything else in your life, learn how to negotiate accepting a job offer.

Forget the flowery speeches and concentrate on knowing the other side's strengths and weaknesses. In other words, do your homework!

- **Get superior information**. That's why car dealers win in negotiations. They know exactly how much they paid for the car they're trying to sell, and also how much your trade-in is worth. Few ordinary car buyers take the time to learn those two critical numbers. And even when they think they know, the dealer throws in variables like options and financing charges that help disguise the dealership's true profit margin. The result is that only the most sophisticated customers know how to cut a deal without cutting their own throats. The true pro salesperson has customers believing they have stolen the car.

- **Don't make decisions for other people**. When you *let* them decide, you *make* them decide. Be clear, friendly, and polite, but don't jump over to the other side of the table if you sense the party with whom you're negotiating is uncomfortable.

- **Stay calm**. If you're tight in the batter's box, you can't hit. Better-than-average hitters always keep a quiet bat until it's time to swing. Pounding the table only works in the movies.

- **Anticipate questions**. Know the answer to every question you might be asked before you sit down at the table, and you won't have to appear as if you are negotiating.

- **Be a spin doctor**. Finesse questions. For example, if you are asked, "What do you need for a salary?" Reply with, "Do you have a salary range established for the position?"

- **Remember, silence is golden**. Do as little negotiating as possible. Make your potential employer make the first offer—it could be a pleasant surprise. On the other hand, if you make the first offer and suggest a number lower than the employer was about to offer you, you're giving him a pleasant surprise.

- **Keep evaluating the employer**. What do you know about his or her needs? How long has he or she been looking? Is this proving to be a tough position to fill? Does this firm have a reputation for being a high payer or a low payer? Is it noted for high or low turnover? Does it tend to provide a fast track or a slow track for its employees? A job search can go on for months, and, as we have all seen, market conditions can gyrate overnight.

- **Keep evaluating yourself**. What bargaining advantage do you hold? Top grades? Explosive potential? Superior past performance? First-rate credentials and experience? Proven skills? Tested and steadfast loyalty? Will it matter to the company if it doesn't hire you and hires someone else instead? Is your future promise of such value to the company that it wouldn't want you to go to the competitor? Can you prove it?

- **In any job search, the tide can shift constantly and it's easy to lose track of a negotiation.** Your counterpart can skillfully maneuver you into a position where you constantly lose ground and never even notice. Document records of each individual encounter and compare positions frequently to detect if you are gaining or losing ground.

Mackay's Moral: *The smartest thing you often can do in a negotiation is keep your mouth shut and your eyes wide open.*

CHAPTER 6:

TIPS FOR
SPECIAL TEAMS

WHEN OVERQUALIFIEDS
SHOULD CONSIDER
DOWNSIZING

If you're willing to compromise on title, and you should be, you may be the answer to a personnel director's prayers. With all the downsizing and cutbacks, companies are having enormous compression problems with titles.

Consider downsizing your title as a trading card. It could be your ace in the hole. Don't throw it away. Hoard it carefully and play it when you need it. It could go a long way toward helping you cut a better deal for yourself.

This is the horse-trading part of the deal. Anticipate every possible area of employer/employee relations you can think of in your pre-sign-up discussions. Then you're way ahead of the game, and you're way ahead of 99 percent of all hires.

Conceding on title is one thing. Downsizing into a smaller job is quite another. True downsizing is often a struggle. And any new employer willing to take you on will be legitimately skeptical of your intentions and your integrity.

Be prepared to demonstrate permanent lifestyle cutbacks. The new job shouldn't seem like a panic trip to a fallout shelter. Be prepared to show how you and your family are meaningfully reducing monthly expenses to live within a new budget. Perhaps the second car goes. Your stay-at-home spouse is now in the market for part-time work. Private education for the kids may be trimmed back to public alternatives. Yes, even the summer cabin may have to go. A new employer may look for strong reassurance that this is a realistic long-term adjustment.

If you felt out of your depth with your former responsibilities, this may be the time to admit it. Perhaps you didn't like the extra weight of management. Maybe you really were aching to a return to those days as a technician or backroom researcher. Companies know that people won't tolerate ego abuse long-term. If you convince them of a credible, revised self-image, that can be a major plus.

Position the move as a calculated transition strategy. Establish what your potential employer's expectations are. Maybe your new prospective employer is only looking for a two-year commitment. Perhaps you will use the two years to train evenings and weekends for a new field of work. Or you only need two years more of employment until you can bridge to pension and retirement benefits. Your chances are much better if you and your employer share a plausible common plan.

A shower of companies—including some giants like General Motors and Citigroup—have downsized to survive. People should enjoy the same right that firms do, but they will only earn it by being tough and credible.

Mackay's Moral: *Sometimes good things come in smaller packages.*

"On my home planet, I was a deity."

BABY BOOMER GLOOM: PROFESSIONAL PEP FOR THOSE 55+

If you're a boomer, don't make 55 your psychological speed limit. We live in a use-it-or-lose-it world. The older we get, the more we have to convince people who are likely to be younger than we are. It's true in selling. It's true in finding a job.

The job market is a high-performance game. You're going for impact, and you won't land a punch if you're not tuned in to today's footwork.

Staying sharp and savvy? It's easier than you think.

- Check out where young people get their information and their entertainment. Stream a top-rated TV show on your tablet. Invest as much attention in the ads as the content. Watch the news on social media, not just CNN or Fox. An amazing number of millennials get their news from Twitter.

- It's quite possible your potential bosses will be younger than you, and their reflexes may be a tad more agile, too. If they're into extreme snowboarding, for instance, you don't have to jib or free carve your way into the orthopedic ward. It still pays to learn a term or two ... and their performance goals.

- If your waistline has become something of a battle-ground and you're interviewing over lunch, nix ordering a trans-fat bombshell. Stay in touch with food and nutrition trends.

- Do you regularly scroll through the *Wired* web-site for the latest phalanx of apps and techno-innovations? Have you played (and graciously lost) Xbox games with your kids or grandkids?

Mackay's Moral: *If you want to stay in the game, you'd better learn the tricks of the trade.*

HOW NON-TECHIES TACKLE
A TECH WORLD

ntimidated by younger people, especially those lithe multi-taskers who know every app and can tickle the keyboard of a smartphone in their sleep?

I won't even get into the "netiquette" of chat rooms to try to dish out their latest lingo. Nor should you. Instead, focus on the high-cred basics that garner awe from every generation. Among them:

- **Know your stuff.** A job candidate is pitching personal credibility. You don't have to know all that much, but say what you do know with resounding accuracy and confidence.

- **If you don't have a clue, don't go there.** Never dish up baloney to a techie. A simple "I don't know"—especially if you think you know, but don't—will likely earn you respect and trust.

- **Don't let your comments wander aimlessly.** Talk orderly-mind-to-orderly-mind and don't flit randomly from one topic to another.

- **Unleash the ingenuity of the employer you want to hire you.** Show them features of yourself that ignite their creative intelligence and will make you exciting and rewarding to be around.

- **Realize newness is an appeal, not a threat.** Show receptivity to new ways of looking at ideas and a willingness to find new ways to apply innovation.
- **Supplement and satisfy insecurities.** Provide reliable dependability and mature wisdom, while displaying an appetite and a key interest in what's new and energizing.

Mackay's Moral: *If the tech world is out of your orbit, you need to showcase your willingness to shoot for the stars.*

GIVING RECENT COLLEGE GRADS A STANDOUT EDGE

~~~

In the past 40 years, I have counseled not hundreds but *thousands* of kids who are college seniors or who have just graduated about how to get a job. Here are 10 tips that capture the gist of what I learned:

- There's *always* an alumni club, and it isn't just for the school that handed you a diploma. It could be the community flood control project for which you piled sandbags three years ago. Maybe you were a spear-carrier in a community theater version of *Titus Andronicus*. Consider every plausible group affiliation when you plan your networking.

- Summer internships can be invaluable, but competition is fierce. Start angling for one at least a year before you hope to land it.

- Always be helpful to people in your network before (maybe y-e-a-r-s before) you impose on people to return a favor.

- As soon as you have an idea of what your career goal will be five years from now, identify a mentor who is where you want to be. Learn everything you can about this person and find ways to create a personal contact. Mentors will change over your career, but this is a smart place to start. Such a person can be invaluable in suggesting early career experiences that could be invaluable but are possibilities you never even considered.

- This suggestion is before you graduate: As soon as you can, try to link some project or research you do in getting your degree with a potential job connection in the future.

- Develop some specialized expertise that could have commercial value to a company as early as you can.

- Do visible not-for-profit work that demonstrates your capabilities. One remarkable young lady I met did volunteer work in Swaziland, hardly a vacation paradise. More than half of the population lives on less than $1.25 a day.

- From a piece in *Wired,* comes this invaluable tip for techies from Thomas Hatch, CTO of Salt Stack, a tech startup in Utah: Do open-source programming. (These are programs that are freely available to the public like Mozilla Firefox, Android and Linux.) Hatch agrees with others who believe that "contributing to open source is one of the best ways to land a job in software. 'It makes it easier to hire technical talent,' Hatch says. 'You can see how someone's evolved—or not evolved—as a developer. We're extremely wary of hiring people who haven't contributed to open source.'"

- Compromise: If you can't find the ideal job as your first job, look for something that could build valuable skills you could lean on later.

- Consider working for free on a self-imposed trial basis with clear terms to prove you're even better than you say you are.

Mackay's Moral: *To get to play in the majors, major in what matters in the modern world.*

CHAPTER 7:

THE TOOLKIT

THE MACKAY SWEET 16 FOR ACING FIRST IMPRESSIONS

Firest impressions are critical.

So are last ones.

The last thing people remember before or as they enter a crisis can shake the stars and unhinge the heavens.

The late Roger Ebert, *Chicago Sun-Times* film critic, courageously battled back from a host of medical trials in the years before he passed away. According to a 2010 *Esquire* article, "There was one song in particular he played over and over [during his medical trials in 2006]: 'I'm Your Man,' by Leonard Cohen. That song saved his life [which extended several more years.]" Cohen's ditty is all about adaptability and resourcefulness.

Remember that last list of unforgettable points you stared at before walking into a huge exam in high school or college?

For decades now, people have asked me the last thing someone should study before going into a key job interview.

I thought of it as my *Last Reminder Survival List.*

Everybody else has come to know it as **Mackay's Sweet 16.**

The easiest thing in the world is for you to settle for what's available. Smart interviewers don't want to know what you'll settle for.

They're after where you want to go.

Is there a huge chasm between your dreams and what this job has to offer? How could any employer conclude you would be motivated to deliver the goods for them?

1. **Be prepared to describe your ideal job:** the position you would most like to have (include title, responsibilities, who you would report to, who would report to you).

2. **Describe your ideal company:** size, industry, culture, location and structure.

3. **Can you articulate clear and realistic future goals?** Where do you want to be in your career in three to five years?

4. **What do you want your next job to do for you that your last job didn't do?** And don't say "last forever"—nothing does.

5. **What kinds of growth should the new job offer (promotions, training, challenges)?** Employees are usually keen on personal growth opportunities that emphasize strengthening your team-playing skills.

6. **What skills will you be able to add to your résumé while you have this job?** Think creatively about how those skills might mesh with the immediate, bottom-line needs of the company with which you are interviewing.

7. **Why should a company want to hire you?** What can you say about yourself that convinces a company they would be missing out on a serious opportunity by **not** putting you on the payroll?

8. **What personal and professional accomplishments are you most proud of?** Keep in mind: Those achievements showcasing the development of other people are big attractions to today's employers.

9. **What do you least want to be asked in an interview—what are the questions you dread most?** These are the questions deserving the best, clearest preparation. Honesty in your answers goes without saying.

10. **How will you handle the tough questions?** Like a polished NFL quarterback handles crunch time. Coolly. Decisively. Smoothly.

11. **What compensation, including salary and benefits, do you want to earn and can you legitimately ask for?** Know thy marketplace!

12. **What are the most important benefits other than salary that would prompt you to work for a new company?** Read that to mean: What short-term challenges facing this company would be invaluable personal development opportunities for you?

13. **What tools and resources can you draw on to help you through your job transition?** And what talents and support people, who are members of your fan club, can you bring to the party?

14. **What can you say in an interview that would really set you apart from other well-suited candidates?** Any intelligence you have on those other candidates—even though you might not be able to mention their names—can be a great power edge.

15. **What could your current employer do for you that would prevent you from looking for another job in the first place? (Have you asked?)** During a recovery, many people assume that the last person to occupy a job left involuntarily. The company may have had a tough time holding on to talent, and it obviously helps to know it. Clearly selling a mature sense of patience always helps.

16. **How will you know when you've become a success?** Find out the measures the prospective company will be using, and never forget the mega-difference between achievement of hard-and-fast goals and significant progress toward their achievement.

In a job interview, you're always selling. You can never sell if (1) you don't constantly anticipate the next question, and (2) the prospect is convinced they have nailed what you are really after.

"I'm Your Man" or "I'm Your Woman" only works if you really mean it.

Mackay's Moral: Sometimes no job is better than a forced job.

THE MACKAY 44 INTERVIEW PREP CHECKLIST

Whether you're new to the game or heading to your hundredth interview, the preparation process is the same. Here is my checklist to help you get organized.

Timing and Advance Planning

1. Scheduling: Try for the time of day you shine best.
2. Get a good night's rest the day before.
3. Try to do a workout in the morning. It will help improve your alertness and relax you.
4. Create a contact sheet for each company with names, phone numbers, email addresses.
5. If a recruiter is involved, have a pre-meeting huddle about positioning for the interview.
6. Review your own videos of your simulated interviews.
7. If any forms are needed, complete them neatly in advance.

Apparel and Appearance

8. Shine shoes, check fingernails.
9. Haircut and styling, comb.

10. Suit and shirt or blouse choice, tie.

11. Accessories (including watch, umbrella, if necessary, etc.).

Reading and Research

12. Recent articles on the prospective company.

13. Company website for their latest news + press releases.

14. Know the company's most recent annual and quarterly sales and profits.

15. Google people you'll be meeting for background on them.

16. Know how to pronounce names of people you will meet.

17. If possible, learn the names of the receptionist and admin assistants.

18. If this is a second interview, review notes of past meetings.

19. Scroll through the day's business news so you have something to talk about.

20. Create a list of good questions you will ask the interviewer.

21. Check emails just before leaving for any last-minute rescheduling.

Take Withs

22. Smartphone (turn off before interview).

23. Portfolio or business case.

24. Résumé copies (at least two).

25. Business cards.

26. Blank paper or notebook + pens.

27. Breath mints or spray.

28. Your personal calendar if a follow-up meeting is discussed.

Getting There

29. Plan on being punctual and intend to arrive several minutes early.

30. Weather report in case you need to plan on extra time.

31. Google map + either pre-drive or investigate road congestion.

32. Parking practices.

33. Correct building entrance?

34. Anticipate going through security and having to wear a visitor badge.

If Meeting Over a Meal

35. Eat something like a power bar or piece of fruit beforehand.

36. If possible, know the menu in advance.

Just Before Showtime

37. Do a once-over in the mirror for hair and clothing.

38. Pay attention to your posture.

39. Have a reasonable idea of appropriate, positive opening comments.

40. Put on a warm, relaxed smile.

41. Prepare for a firm handshake.

Plan Follow-up in Advance

42. Plan in advance how and where you will debrief yourself.

43. Have stationery and postage ready for handwritten thank-you notes.

44. If a recruiter is involved, know how to reach this person after the interview for a debriefing.

———

Mackay's Moral: *The difference is in the details. Prepare thoroughly to perform admirably.*

THE MACKAY 22
POST-INTERVIEW WRAP-UP

A fter a job interview, do you know what happens in the office of the recruiter, personnel manager or boss you just visited? They close the door and record or type into their tablet, smartphone or notebook. They pass judgment on your future. Said differently: They do their homework, grading your performance.

I'm astonished at how few job candidates take their own futures seriously enough to do the same. They don't record or organize their notes on interviews that potentially have such an impact on their lives.

If you're going to put your future and your fate in anyone's hands, it should be your own. You have your own evaluations to make. These include impressions about your performance in the interview and about the company as a possible employer.

The job interview is a corporate ritual, and your role in this mating dance is not to take control, but to react intelligently and creatively to the signals you get from your interviewer. Getting the job is always going to be your number-one priority, but getting the answers to the questions about the job is right up there as a close second.

Simple discipline. Basic questions. But for my money, simple and basic are the only way to go. This is so important,

I'd fill it out even before I wrote the thank-you note to the interviewer!

Here's a sampling of the information you should gather:

1. Date of Interview: Name of firm. Phone number. Address. Interviewer. Title.
2. Describe position being filled.
3. Last person left job because ...
4. Position reports to: Title: And, who reports to this position?
5. Key duties of job.
6. If last person in job succeeded, *why?* If last person in job failed, *why?*
7. Chances to get ahead? Describe: Can you move laterally within the company to other departments requiring other skills? Describe: Does the company encourage educational and training programs? Describe.
8. Would relocation be necessary now? In the future? Probable?
9. Describe the "ideal" candidate.
10. Important information about pay, benefits, etc.
11. When can you expect a decision? Was the interviewer specific? Vague?
12. Five most important questions you were asked?
13. Three most difficult or embarrassing questions?
14. What three things did the interviewer seem to like most about you or your background?

15. What reservations or concerns did the interviewer reveal? What did you say or do during the interview that you wished you hadn't?

16. New company information you learned that you might be able to use later?

17. How would this job/company be a good fit? How would it be a poor fit?

18. Did you mention any references? Which ones? Have you alerted these people?

19. How did the interviewer describe your potential boss?

20. Is this the kind of person you would trust? Feel comfortable working with?

21. Any special conditions under which you might be offered the job? Did you mention any conditions for you to accept it?

22. Fresh from the interview, what would be the biggest attraction to you in taking this job? The biggest drawback?

As I've said, complete the form as soon as possible after your interview, while the information is still fresh in your mind. Then use it as a reference tool as you move along toward getting the job you've always wanted.

A backup gambit to remember in a jam: Chances are every interview will include some question that was a bit too technical for you to answer. When someone spears you with a gotcha question, you can be the perfect New Age team player. Consider saying: "That's a great question. I don't remember just now, but I know a woman who's a whiz on Pinterest. Shall I text her and see if she's there?" Everybody needs lifelines. If you don't know it yourself, be ready to show how well you can network to an answer. Hey, you didn't watch all those hours of "Who Wants to Be a Millionaire?" for nothing!

***

Mackay's Moral: *Pale ink is better than the most retentive memory.*

FOLLOW YOUR PASSION

Maybe it's time to reconsider your options. Are you sure you want a job in the same industry? Have you thought about trying your hand at a different career?

Tim practiced law, quite successfully, for more than 30 years. His practice included representing defendants who had some tough breaks growing up and followed the wrong path as they grew into adulthood. "Story after story was the same sad situation—absent parents, no motivation to do well in school, little supervision, basically no encouragement. It started to occur to me that I could have done more for them at an earlier point in their lives than I could with all my legal training and experience," he said.

So, Tim decided that "early retirement" for him would mean a return to college to get a teaching degree, and he would concentrate his job search in some of the poorest neighborhood schools in his city. His student teaching semester almost did him in. "I understand what challenges teachers must overcome even before they have their students crack open their books," he said. "I am determined to let every one of my students know that if they are willing to do the work, I am willing to be their biggest cheerleader. And I love every minute of it."

By the way, Tim made that move seven years ago and he's still going strong. He also admits, "I changed careers at just the right time. Don't get me wrong: I loved practicing law and I was very good at it. But I have found that you can have more than one passion in your work life, and I am incredibly fortunate to have discovered that."

Maureen owns an art supply store. She is an unlikely entrepreneur: a former nurse who enjoyed painting as a hobby but admits her work will probably never warrant an exhibition. She had a perfect work schedule, working at a hospital three days a week with hours that made it possible for her to be available for her kids' activities and accommodate family schedules. She was highly satisfied with her career, liked her hospital and coworkers, provided excellent care for her patients, and could have stayed in that routine with no regrets.

Then Maureen inherited a few thousand dollars from a relative, which got her thinking about what she should do with that money. In the back of her mind, she had always thought it might be fun to be the proprietor of a little store where artists would hang out and discuss their current work, find inspiration for new projects and buy their supplies.

After considerable thought and consultation with folks in the business and her bank, Maureen decided to leave the hospital and leased a small storefront. She has since expanded twice and has to fight the temptation to open a second site. "I love opening my little shop every morning, knowing that I built this business and that my customers trust me to take good care of them—not so different from my nursing days!" she said.

I heard so many of these stories. Some career changers went for a variation of a theme, like the interior designer who got her real estate license and is in great demand for the high-end clients who appreciate her eye for the details. Others took great leaps, like the insurance executive who went to cosmetology school with the eventual intention of owning a funky salon.

Some were burned out by their current careers; others downsized out of their jobs. Some had put dreams aside for more practical occupations. Still others had settled into the first job they were offered, until it occurred to them that they didn't really like what they were doing for a living.

Like I've always said, find a job you love, and you'll never work another day in your life.

Mackay's Moral: *Don't be afraid to take the plunge —just test the water before you dive in!*

ABOUT THE AUTHOR

Harvey Mackay has written seven *New York Times* bestselling books, three reached #1, and two were named by the *Times* among the top 15 inspirational business books of all time: *Swim With the Sharks Without Being Eaten Alive* and *Beware the Naked Man Who Offers You His Shirt.*

Harvey's latest book is *You Haven't Hit Your Peak Yet!*, debuted on Jan. 29, 2020. His other books include *The Mackay MBA of Selling in the Real World* (November 2011), *Use Your Head to Get Your Foot in the Door: Job Search Secrets No One Else Will Tell You* (2010), *We Got Fired! ... And It's the Best Thing That Ever Happened To Us* (2004), *Pushing the Envelope* (1999), and *Dig Your Well Before You're Thirsty: The Only Networking Book You'll Ever Need* (1997). His books have sold 10 million copies in 80 countries and have been translated in 52 languages.

For the last 27 years, Harvey has been a nationally syndicated columnist. His weekly articles appear in 100 newspapers and magazines around the country, including the *Minneapolis Star Tribune and the Arizona Republic.*

He is one of America's most popular and entertaining business speakers for Fortune 500-size companies and associations, and has spoken on six continents. Toastmasters International named him one of the top five speakers in the world, and he is a member of the National Speakers Association Hall of Fame.

In addition, Harvey is chairman of MackayMitchell Envelope Company, a $100 million company he founded at age 26. MackayMitchell has 400 employees and manufactures 25 million envelopes a day.

Harvey is a graduate of the University of Minnesota and the Stanford University Graduate School of Business Executive Program. He is an avid runner and marathoner, having run 10 marathons, and is a former #1 ranked senior tennis player in Minnesota.

The American Management Association listed Harvey among the top 30 leaders who influenced business in 2014, which also included Colin Powell, Jack Welch, and Richard Branson. In July 2015, Forbes said, "Harvey Mackay is one of the world's top leadership experts who has accomplished more in business than most entrepreneurs could achieve in their lifetimes."

In April 2004, Harvey received the prestigious Horatio Alger Award in the Supreme Court Chambers. Previous recipients include Presidents Eisenhower, Ford, and Reagan, former Secretary of State Colin Powell and entertainer Oprah Winfrey.

He was inducted into the Minnesota Business Hall of Fame in 2002. He is the past president of the Minneapolis Chamber of Commerce, the Envelope Manufacturers Association of America, the University of Minnesota National Alumni Association, to name only a few. In October 2008, he was presented the University of Minnesota Outstanding Achievement Award, the highest award presented to an alumnus.

He played a key role in bringing the 1992 Super Bowl to Minneapolis, along with serving as the catalyst in bringing an NBA franchise (Minnesota Timberwolves) to his home state, serving as chairman of the task force in getting the Hubert H. Humphrey Metrodome built, recruiting Lou Holtz to coach the University of Minnesota football team, and many more.

All of which is why Fortune magazine refers to him as "Mr. Make Things Happen."

CLOSING THOUGHTS

If you have thoughts, comments, or ideas about this book, I'd love to hear from you. (Please, no requests for personal advice.)

Write to me at the following address:

Harvey Mackay
MackayMitchell Envelope Company
2100 Elm St. SE
Minneapolis, MN 55414

You can reach me at my email: harvey@mackay.com or my website, www.harveymackay.com.

INDEX